The GIFT of the BROKEN TEACUP

Poems of Mindfulness, Meditation, and Me

ALLAN WOLF

illustrated by
JADE ORLANDO

CANDLEWICK PRESS

THE GIFT OF THE BROKEN TEACUP

I drink my tea
from a broken cup.
The handle is gone,
so I pick the cup up
with both hands cupped
as if to pray.
I've learned my tea
tastes better this way.

BECAUSE I HAVE INTEGRITY

When I do something wrong,
                    I will right it.
When a battle is just,
                    I will fight it.
When the floor needs a sweeping,
                    I'll sweep it.
When I make you a promise,
                    I'll keep it.
When I borrow a toy,
                    I'll return it.
When I want to have something,
                    I'll earn it.
And that's why you can trust in me:
because I have integrity.

I'LL BE BACK TOMORROW

I punch a pad and jam my thumb.
I kick a bag and stub my toe.
My form feels bad. My jumps feel dumb.
I'll still be back tomorrow, though.
Yes, I'll be back tomorrow.

My belt slips down around my knees.
I keep forgetting moves I know!
I'm sore and sort of ill at ease.
I'll still be back tomorrow, though!
Yes, I'll be back tomorrow!

The most important thing I've learned
since I started tae kwon do
is *Don't give up no matter what.*
You won't arrive if you don't go.
So I'll be back tomorrow. Oh
yes, I'll be back tomorrow!

INDOMITABLE SPIRIT

On rainy days I am the sun.
> Indomitable spirit.
When I do chores, I make them fun.
> Indomitable spirit.
I don't give up until I'm done.
> Indomitable spirit!

I smile although I may feel sad.
I see the good within the bad.
Forgive instead of getting mad.
> Indomitable spirit!

Sometimes I'm down but not for long.
> Indomitable spirit!
I don't give up when things go wrong.
> Indomitable spirit!
When I feel weak, I come on strong.
> Indomitable spirit!

Determination in my eye,
I say hello to passersby.
And they smile back because of my . . .
> indomitable spirit!

NOT JUST ME

I say, "Hello there! How are you?"
I let you talk, and listen to
whatever you might have to say
before I talk about my day.

I say kind things: "I love your hat!"
I open doors: "Let me get that!"

I'm thoughtful: "Look, I made you this!"
I'm giving: "Would you like my chips?"
I say "Excuse me" when I burp.
When I eat soup, I do not slurp.

And that's how I show courtesy:
I think of others, not just me.

INCONSEQUENTIAL

inconsequential (adjective): unimportant, worthless

Most things inconsequential
go unmentioned in the news.
But a ray inconsequential
makes a rainbow's many hues.
A flame inconsequential
lights a firecracker fuse.
And a thought inconsequential
may become a poet's muse.

A breeze inconsequential
keeps a bird aloft in flight.
A cry inconsequential
wakes a mother up at night.
A dog inconsequential
is a forest for a flea.
Your inconsequential
may mean everything to me.

And my inconsequential
may mean all the world to you.
Always try to see things
from another's point of view.

IMAGINATION MOVES AWAY

The pirate ship is derelict,
abandoned on the sea.
The garden is deserted,
flowers withered into weeds.
The tire swing spins slowly
as its lonely rope unravels.
The secret trail is thick with leaves.
The quest is left untraveled.
The jungle gym is choked with vines.
The tree fort stands alone.
Imagination moved away;
the children have all grown.

BE YOU THE BREAD

If you're not being fed,
then be you the bread
     and set out your table for others.

Your guests will be grateful,
and those who are able
     will share their own jelly and butter.

The meals we deserve
are the ones that we serve,
     no matter if portions are small.

If you're not being fed,
then be you the bread
     and offer your goodness to all.

CALLING ALL HUMANITY: YOU HAVE WON THE LOTTERY!

Calling all humanity!
You have won the lottery!
Go outside. Emerge and see
the birds, the bees,
the clouds, the trees,
the winter chill,
the summer breeze,
the springtime blooms
the falling leaves.
If only you emerge and see,
you'll see you've won the lottery.

Calling all humanity!
Just contemplate the mystery
of how you even came to be!

You could have been fleas on the hairs of a dog.
You could have been warts on an angry baboon.
You could have been coffee stains left on the carpet.
You could have been timpani played out of tune.
You could have been fungus attached to a log.
You could have been slime from a toxic lagoon.

You could have been tar in a bubbling tar pit
on some other galaxy's planet or moon.

Instead, all those molecules merged in a stew,
making eight billion humans—including one YOU!
And one you.
And one you.
And one you.
And me, too!

Calling all humanity:
you have won the lottery!
Walk out the door. Emerge and see:
of all the possibilities
of time and space and galaxies,
not only to exist, but be
aware of it, and know that we,
and every other you and me,
the entirety of humanity—
we've all won the lottery!

YAWP!

I sound my barbaric yawp over the roofs of the world.
—Walt Whitman

A poet named Whitman
(his friends called him Walt)
inspired the world
with his barbaric YAWP!
A word that's a joyous,
heartfelt celebration.
A birthday, bar mitzvah,
and summer vacation
all packed into one small
splendiferous word.

So try it yourself,
loud enough to be heard!
Let it spring out
like a jack-in-the-box.

Pretend you're a mountain—
your mouth is the top—
and sound out your very own
barbaric YAWP!

YAWP!

I'M WORKING ON MY PhD IN HOW TO STAND BENEATH A TREE

I'm working on my PhD
in how to stand beneath a tree
at Blue Ridge University
of Mountain Meditating.

No laptop, GPS, or phone.
My classroom is a trail unknown.
My teacher whispers, "Welcome home.
The forest has been waiting."

A soft snow cloaks the woods in white.
Ahead. Behind. To left and right.
No creature large or small in sight.
The world is hibernating.

As snowflakes fill the winter sky,
inside my chest, spring arrives.
And all at once I realize
my soul is germinating.

I'm working on my PhD
in how to stand beneath a tree
at Blue Ridge University
of Mountain Meditating.

I'm *never* graduating.

HOW TO MEDITATE

No sound.

Sit down.

Crisscross.

Applesauce.

Quiet ease.

Hands on knees.

Palms up.

Fingers touch.

Close eyes.

Soft sighs.

Sit tall.

That's all.

MY MIND'S EYE IS A CLEAR BLUE SKY

To meditate, I close my eyes
and gaze into my mind's blue sky,
where I can see my thoughts pass by
like clouds, or birds, or butterflies.
These thoughts I see aren't part of me.
I watch them crossing silently.
Hello. Goodbye. I leave them be
to pass me by and set me free
from *What?* And *When?* And *How?* And *Why?*
My mind's eye is a clear blue sky.

THE OM POEM

An *om* is an *o*
with an *m* at the end.
When practicing yoga,
it's how we begin.
It's deep and it's long.
It's the very best way
to start meditation
or greet the new day.
An *om* is a poem
without any words.
It acts as a voice
so the heart can be heard.
An *om* resonates
through your tummy and toes.

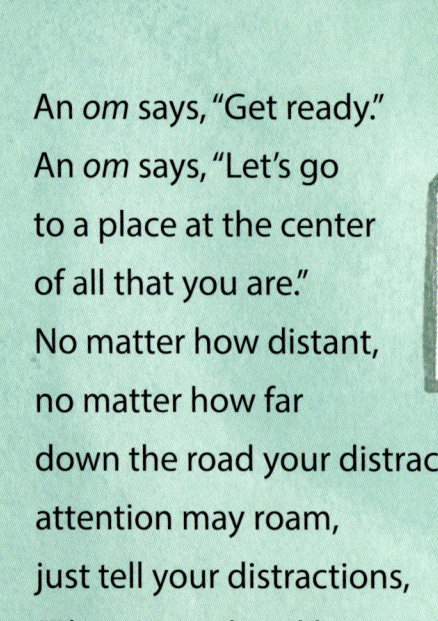

An *om* says, "Get ready."
An *om* says, "Let's go
to a place at the center
of all that you are."
No matter how distant,
no matter how far
down the road your distracted
attention may roam,
just tell your distractions,
"There's no place like *om*."

TO BE INVISIBLE AS AIR

Inside my heart, there is a place
where I can visit to escape
and meditate my mind away.
No work to do. No words to say.
I play a quiet breathing song.
Forever mine and never wrong.
My two legs folded under me,
I sit in wonder, silently,
to be invisible as air,
a still and barely whispered prayer.
I look, but I don't use my eyes.
And when I'm finished, then I rise.
A smile spreads out across my face.
And from that place where I escape,
my private heart-songs resonate.

BUTTERFLY MEDITATION

Lie down on your back.

       Close your eyes.

Imagine that a butterfly

      flutters just above you there.

           Its wings stir up the gentle air.

             Imagine, now, it softly lands

         upon your fingers

           then your hand.

         Now feel it land upon your nose,

         your eyelids,

            belly,

               knees,

                and toes.

Now watch it as it gently goes

up, up, up to touch the ceiling,

leaving you a gentle feeling

from hand to hand and head to toe.

Now open eyes.

           Now sit up slow.

Now give your butterfly a name.

Say, "Thank you, friend.

         I'm glad you came."

YOGA

tabula rasa (noun): a blank slate, a new beginning

Yoga is breathing and balance and strength.
Yoga is "Slow down,"
                    "Let go,"
          and
                    "Give thanks."

Yoga is downward dog, pigeon, and tree.
Straighten your spine while supporting your chi.

Flowing and stretching and holding each pose.
Reaching up high. Folding over your toes.

Your muscles and mind in polite conversation.
Your body and brain in a collaboration.

Yoga is closing your eyes to vinyasa
and opening them to a tabula rasa.

From Sun Salutation to deep relaxation.
A boost!
          A rebirth!
                    And a rejuvenation!

STANDING MEDITATION STRETCH

Inhale very slowly through your nose.

    Exhale very slowly through your mouth.

Inhale through your nose and reach the sky.

    Exhale through your mouth and give a sigh.

Inhale through your nose and fold your wings.

    Exhale through your mouth and softly sing.

Inhale as you slowly turn around.

    Exhale through your mouth as you sit down.

When feeling restless, stand up straight,

    and then repeat lines one through eight.

WALKING MEDITATION

Heel, toe.
Heel, toe.
Walking meditation.

Heel, toe.
Smooth flow.
Walking meditation.

Heel, toe.
Sloth slow.
Walking meditation.

Deep breaths
through nose.
Walking meditation.

Thoughts come.
Thoughts go.
Walking meditation.

Turn around.
No sound.
Walking meditation.

Lift feet.
Repeat.
Walking meditation.

Heel, toe.
Heal woe.
Walking meditation.

WIDE AWAKE?
FOUR-SEVEN-EIGHT!

Lights are out? It's getting late?
But your body's wide awake?
Inhale as you count to four.
Hold your breath for seven more.
Exhale slowly counting eight.
Inhale, counting four, then wait.
Hold again for seven more.
Sail away to slumber's shore.
Exhale slow and inhale deep.
Hold and count. Repeat. Repeat.
Repeat until you fall asleep.

me

I'M THE ONE IN CHARGE OF ME

Sometimes it's up to me to be
the only one in charge of me.

I try my best to concentrate.
I sit still while I meditate.

I say, "Yes, sir!" I say, "Yes, ma'am!"
I line up quickly as I can.

I wait my turn and raise my hand
whenever I don't understand.

I practice without being told.
And that's how I show self-control.

Sometimes it's up to me to be
the one who is in charge of me.

YOU BE YOU

Just be yourself with all your flaws.
Don't act like someone else, because
if you were them and they were you,
your pants and shirts and socks and shoes
would be too baggy, or too tight,
instead of fitting you just right.
Just think how happy we will be
if you're just you and I'm just me.
So you be you and no one else.
Don't try to be someone who isn't
yourself.

BETSY BEST, MY WORST BEST FRIEND

Betsy Best is my best friend
because she knows what's best.
But lately Betsy Best has put
our friendship to the test.

I say, "My desk is messy."
Betsy says, "My desk is messier!"
I say, "My dress is dressy."
Betsy says, "My dress is dressier!"

I say, "My hair is wavy."
Betsy says, "My hair is wavier!"
I say, "I'm well-behaved."
Betsy says, "I'm well-behaved-ier!"

I say, "I feel terrific."
Betsy says, "I feel terrific-er!"
I say, "I'm scientific."
Betsy says, "I'm scientific-er!"

Don't get me wrong; I'm glad that she
is such a special friend to me.
I only wish my best friend were
a little bit best-friendlier.

I WRITE MYSELF DOWN!

I write me down.

    I write me down.

I write myself down.

I write myself upon the page,
one pen in hand, ten years of age.
I write myself, and as I write,
I write myself to life.

I write myself from head to toe.

I catch a word. I let it grow.

I write down who I wanna be,

a recipe to make a me.

I write myself in simile:

My craft is smooth like mac 'n' cheese.

I write myself in metaphor:

My words, they soar.

My rhythms roar.

I told you all before . . .

I write me down.

    I write me down.

I write myself down.

I write me down.

    I write me down.

        I write me down.

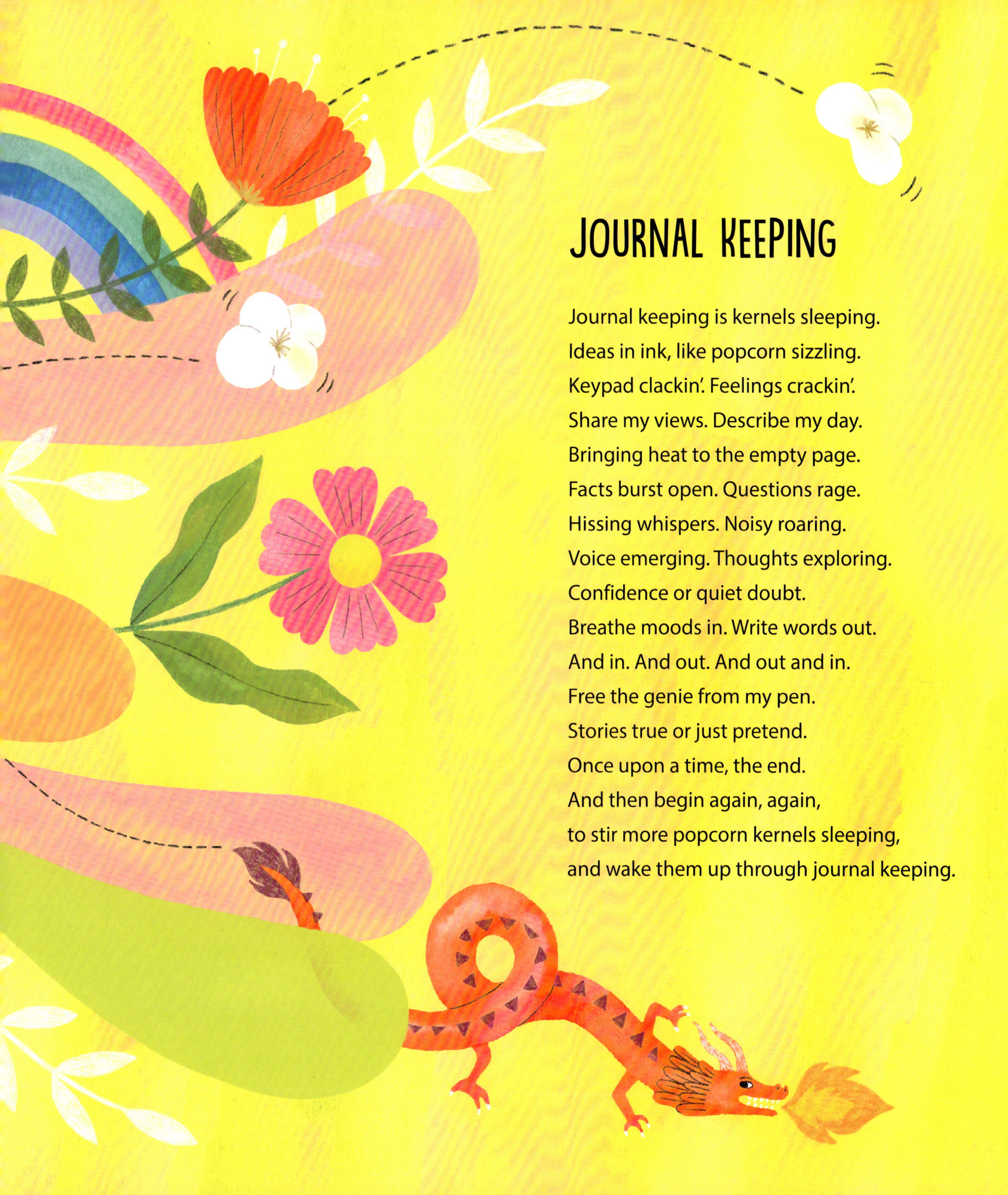

JOURNAL KEEPING

Journal keeping is kernels sleeping.

Ideas in ink, like popcorn sizzling.

Keypad clackin'. Feelings crackin'.

Share my views. Describe my day.

Bringing heat to the empty page.

Facts burst open. Questions rage.

Hissing whispers. Noisy roaring.

Voice emerging. Thoughts exploring.

Confidence or quiet doubt.

Breathe moods in. Write words out.

And in. And out. And out and in.

Free the genie from my pen.

Stories true or just pretend.

Once upon a time, the end.

And then begin again, again,

to stir more popcorn kernels sleeping,

and wake them up through journal keeping.

HOW TO TURN WORRY INTO WONDER

If thinking of the future
makes you anxious and excited
and nervous tummy butterflies
have moved in uninvited,
remember that most worries
are just physical sensations.
So get those bumbling butterflies
all flying in formation.
When worry and anxiety
tear all your world asunder,
accept the way you feel,
then turn that worry into wonder!

The new school year is coming up
with goldfish, glue, and glitter!
Your stomach feels all tangled up
with butterflies and jitters.
You worry that your first big day
will be your next big blunder!
Accept the way you feel,
then turn that worry into wonder!
I wonder what the year will bring.
I wonder what good friends I'll see.
I wonder what fun songs I'll sing.
I wonder what cool books I'll read.
I wonder if we'll laugh a lot.
I wonder if we'll play.
I wonder if an astronaut
will come on Speaker's Day.

When worry and anxiety
tear all your world asunder,
accept the way you feel, and turn
your worry into wonder!
Most fears, and frets, and worries
are just physical sensations.
So get those bumbling butterflies
all flying in formation.

ANGRY? ACT IT OUT!

A: Accept your feelings
C: Choose a positive way
T: Take action

Feelings come to you as gifts.
Accept them and be grateful,
even if those feelings may
seem negative or hateful.

Accept them, but then let them go,
by choosing some creative way
to turn bad feelings upside down
and ACT your angry mood away.

Juggle socks and close your eyes.
Hold your breath and count to five.
Sing a song about your dog or cat.
Draw a tiger, tree, or truck.
Write a poem about a duck.
Tell a joke and wear a fancy hat.
Put a play on with a friend.
Take a bow and, in the end,
you'll start to feel much better—
that's a fact.

When anger gets the best of you,
three simple steps will see you through:
Accept your feelings.
Choose a way.
Then act!

LET IT GO

Don't carry anger. Let it go—
for it will prove a heavy load,
the longer down that road you go.

The longer down that road you go,
the more bent over you become.
Then, by the time your journey's done,
you'll be no use to anyone.

You'll be no use to anyone,
with anger bent and facing down,
your gaze forever toward the ground,
while all about you joy abounds.

While all about you joy abounds,
you'll only see the dirt below.
You'll shuffle blindly down that road
with crooked back and naught to show.

With crooked back and naught to show,
you've got to let the anger go.
You'll miss the joy that's all around
if you don't set your anger down.

Don't carry anger. Let it go.

EVERYTHING CHANGES

Today may bring joy.
Today may bring sorrow.
Tomorrow may shine.
Tomorrow may rain.

But
tomorrow your sorrow
will turn about-face
and turn all your tears
into laughter again.

Whatever the drama,
whatever the weather,
the best will get worse
and the worst will get better.

For Time reassembles,
and Time rearranges;
Time says, "Don't worry, kid.
Everything changes."

THE VERY BEST DAY OF THE YEAR

Carpe diem: Seize the day

My favorite, special, most glad-to-see day,
the day I consider the best.
The day when I really get carried away.
The best day of all. Can you guess?

It isn't my birthday. It isn't Thanksgiving.
It's not Eid,
Hanukkah,
Christmas,
and all.
It's not Halloween that makes life so worth living.
My day happens spring,
summer,
winter,
and fall.

Give up?
Here's the answer: My day is . . .

today!

No waiting in line and no dreary delay.
What yesterday was and tomorrow will be.
Today is the day I'm most happy to see.

So let's make it special. Let's make it new-made.
Let's make it a bass drum and have a parade.
Let's dance it.
        Let's sing it.
                Let's give it a cheer!
Today is the very best day of the year.
What yesterday was and tomorrow will be.
Today is the day that's been waiting for me.

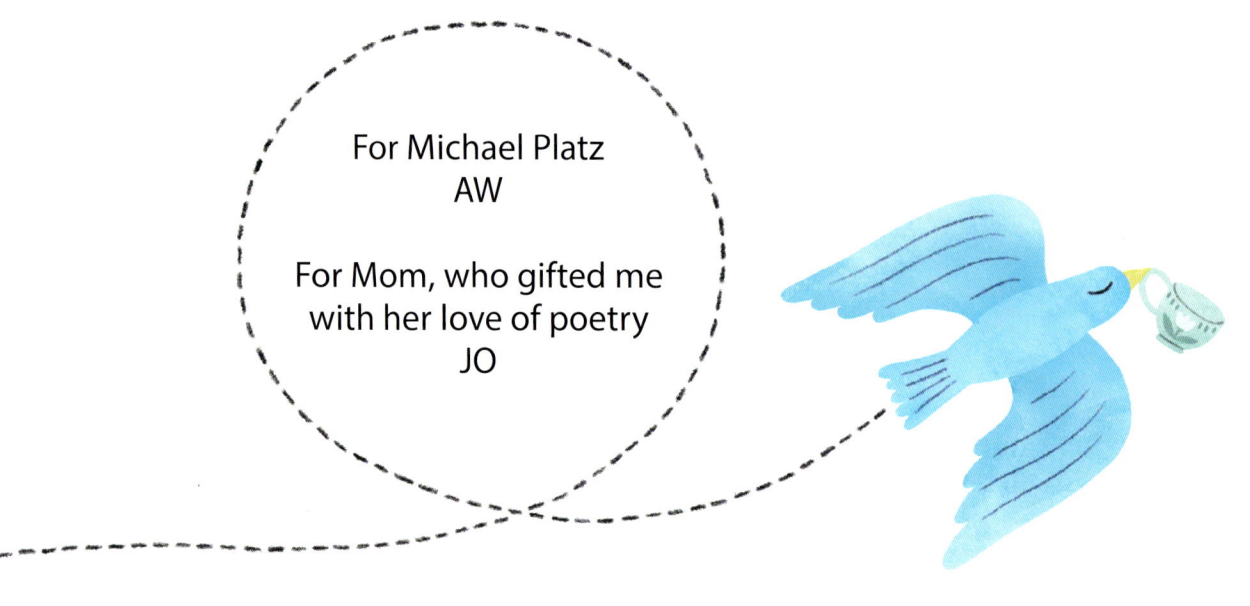

For Michael Platz
AW

For Mom, who gifted me
with her love of poetry
JO

First edition 2025

Library of Congress Catalog Card Number pending
ISBN 978-1-5362-2895-3

25 26 27 28 29 30 CCP 10 9 8 7 6 5 4 3 2 1

Printed in Shenzhen, Guangdong, China

This book was typeset in Myriad Pro.
The illustrations were done in mixed media with digital rendering.

Candlewick Press
99 Dover Street
Somerville, Massachusetts 02144

www.candlewick.com

EU Authorized Representative: HackettFlynn Ltd.,
36 Cloch Choirneal, Balrothery, Co. Dublin, K32 C942, Ireland.
EU@walkerpublishinggroup.com